Introduction

I enjoy writing.

I would like to begin by saying that I am confident that my understanding of what "writing" really is- will continue to change. I won't go as far as to say that it will "develop", as that has far too much of a progressive connotation.

At its core, I believe that the concept of communication is what truly fascinates me. More specifically, for writing, it would be the permanence and the permeance of writing - the capacity for it to have such expansive and yet deep reach, while maintaining a potential for "forever".

Writing has no real rules and it knows no real bounds. (Please tell me more about passive voice and how _weak_ it is). Growing up I marveled at the notion that the better you got at writing - the less you really worried about "correctness". The grammar rules offer guidelines to help ensure communicability of your writing, but at the end of the day it boils down to, simply, your ability to convey the exact thoughts you have to the exact audience you desire - whatever and whomever that is.

I always felt the need to be overly captivating in writing. If your content wasn't dramatically mesmerizing or intellectually fascinating - you couldn't be a good writer. I found myself overly romanticizing even the most basic of emotions in an effort to be more interesting. That was simply it- you had to be _interesting_.
But one of the greatest lessons I learned in life is to appreciate. There is no more to that sentence for a reason - the lesson is simply to appreciate. Subject irrelevant and context immaterial - regardless appreciation.

Anyone who tells you _how_ to write is always both correct and wrong. But maybe I am just a poor writer who has no concept of what "writing" truly entails. In all fairness, this is entirely plausible. All I know is that I appreciate writing and enjoy it. And for me, that is satisfactory.

I find beauty in the vulnerability that comes with writing. All genuine writing is an open door into the mind of the author. I always felt that good writers, particularly those who write a lot, often grow distant from society, yet somehow in doing so also become much more effective in directly communicating to society.

But is it not equally, if not more so, vulnerable to read? To read is to allow a potentially unreliable narrator to guide your thoughts down an unknown road with and unknown destination. Throughout this journey you can only rely on your intuition to hold you true to any thoughts you had prior to reading. You have absolutely no idea of what ideas may invade your mind nor of what effects these ideas may have!

Anyways, I hope you enjoy what is written here – take from it what you will, as this is simply me writing to write.
Enjoy it in any way you choose to.

All written works denoted with a (S) were initially written as pieces of Spoken Word

Things That Were Written

Prince J. Mozart

Table of Contents

Those Who Don't Like Poetry

Those who claim to not like poetry

have simply not found poetry

or are lying to themselves

Time Sensitive

Just got out a 3-year car ride
Could've been a 2-hour flight
With maybe a 20 min break
A Layover 'for leaving the golden state

For the Record (S)

Never have I claimed that I could wreck her

'cause on my record she can see

And after, she can recollect the legacy

Connect the dots, piece together that

I'm her fantasy, she wishes to be, together

Whether with me now or simply for me.

Ignore me she cannot, she simply does adore me

Ride your Bloodline Home

Like a battle on a train

Let it rattle on your brain

Put a saddle on your vein

Ride your Bloodline home

Neglect

I know I've been neglecting you

Subjecting you

To do the things you haven't elected to

Villain

But am I a villain for not wearing the colors of my flag on my chest?

Everyone's has attitude, but do you have personality?

Movement in the public eye, seeking havoc by fatality

If I am, that is the purpose

You can ask all the right questions

But I won't have the answers

It Shows

They unload live rounds on
The road to the high grounds
The road that erodes
Foes will know
That what eats me up inside implodes
Once I let go, of the morals
It shows.

Thinking Out Loud (S)

The say we find things most often where we never tend to
look
I'm sorry it took me a second, but I could write a book on
apologies
So, I'll give that a rest.
We know how this tale starts, and they can guess the rest,
the remainder
I'll tell you the one thing I've come to know -
Even the oldest among us has lived for just the moments
Let me take this moment here to just think out loud
And maybe, just maybe, you can see what I have found

Time will pass, the winds will blow, and many things may
change
But none will rearrange the order of
Look, watch, fall and keep watching
Because that's all I seem to do when you're walking though

26 Letters

Over time, I will write you twenty-six letters

To capture my thoughts and reactions in permanence

But mostly to allow you to say whatever you want in English

A Letter to Whom It May Concern (S)

You don't need my forgiveness, to be frank it does not matter

It wouldn't be too much of a stretch for me to say that I wasn't surprised

I mean, I'm far from perfect and I'm half you

Like a tattoo I can't remove, I see you in a lot that I do

Like telepathy I find empathy rooted in my own thoughts that let me see

But I have no sympathy and I guess that's where I've drawn the line this time

Because at least with what's mine, I would never let her find

Anything that would cause her to lose her peace of mind.

I've decided to keep my mouth closed, not leak any of my deeply planted secret,

Not for your sake but for theirs.

I will shoulder whatever burden you ask of me, but their ignorance truly is bliss

Don't you dare shatter that for them.

You can do whatever you want, just don't bring them down

I shouldn't be the one telling you, but my tongue has always spoken up, nothing new

It's different, the world you're living in, you've made a decision, so deal with it

Care just a little more, feel just a little more, just be responsible and let them be.

They are simply lovers, who need little for satisfaction, you owe them that.

You've created an overly independent fool, but one with a big enough back

And I promise I'll pick up the slack and capture whatever it is that they may lack

I can go harder than you can possibly comprehend –

With or without you, I will keep their dream alive.

This all is not said in anger, but with resolution.

Secrets (S)

she said I've got secrets.

She says I've got them flying around my head

Dippin' through at a thousand miles per hour

The thing is, Truth is, all my secrets are dead.

Ripped through with mental anguish 'n power.

Nothing hidden, fully exposed. Fully disclosed

Like this poem, quickly composed

Inside of me, you'll see no animosity

Possibly a little stress from poverty

Admittedly probably some hypocrisy

But I got no feelings I need to get off of me

The workings of this world truly don't bother me

I got my eyes on the prize - monopoly,

I shoot for the stars - astrology, and time will do its work - chronology.

So, don't fret, don't trip, and most of all don't quit.

'Cause the problems in this world, aren't shit

The goblins and the trolls can't fit

So, you can confess to

Having anger towards everyone reaching success

Nonetheless, I will attest to progress through the stress

Pass through all tests, because I am blessed, I will be the best.

We aren't just mouthing the words, we are rooftop shouting the verbs

The birds will hear, and hold them dear,

For sheer fear of inspiration is near. I am here

Thoughts on Relationships (S)

Now recently, I've done me some thinking.

Something that matters, that's close to me

It's the idea of a relationship, and what it means to be

In one.

I used to say, it was all about expectations,

Expectations of me, and expectations of you

Allowing myself to have any expectations too.

Then when we fail to meet these expectations, we fail

Our 'relationship' crumbles, you cry, I yell, and we fight – we know what that entails

So maybe relationships aren't about expectations, maybe they are just why they fall apart

As cliché as it may be, but maybe it's just a connection of the heart

I realize now that relationships are just being able to be happy with each other.

For her to find pleasure in simply my pleasure, and for me to find joy with her being happy

We may end up doing things I've never thought I would, and find surprising happiness

Long story short, that's all a relationship is to me

I didn't realize that, and that makes up my relationship history

Maybe I used them, and they used me

And we somehow found a little joy in-between.

Where Things Lie

It's funny how what lies before us, also means what is right ahead of us

But what lies inside us, can guide us, if we hold it close beside us

But what lies we hold within, as we bold the wind

Carpe Diem (S)

I proposed to today, hoped to make it mine

Committed to me, forever at a time

You can have the past, the yesterday, and okay

she can borrow the future, the tomorrow

But today is mine, carpe diem

This time, I'll take the worlds before you see 'em, and me um

I got eyes, you can't read 'em

Heartbeats

Feelings come and go,

Thoughts often disappear

My greatest fear, though

Is that my pen can't keep up with my heartbeats

Shell of a Man

Behind every superman is Clark Kent, and he may not admit it, but he isn't as strong

But maybe he won't cry, and make you deal with his issues

And when father time get tough, he'll beat 'em down with mother nature as he bolds the wind with what he is

a strong, invincible, shell... of a man

But he was one, one hell of a fella.

Heavy Shoulders (S)

You tell me that - some days it seems that there is no end

But things are not always as they seem

Some men still do chase dreams

And live *full* vivacious lives through meager means

Your heavy shoulders can carry more weight than

Even colossal boulders can bury with hate

They say its only darkest before light,

But I don't believe in that, its darkest when you close your eyes

Keep your eyes up and stay bright

And together we can walk the night into the daylight

Scarred hearts will heal, and no chain is inescapable

If willing, of greatness you are still capable

For this too shall pass

So, hold it down like I know you can

Battle (S)

Somewhere in the deepest of valleys, in the creases of my mind, a battle rages

A tale scribbled on torn weathered discolored pages

A decrepit old swordsman of the past musters his strength

To remind a fresh face the lessons of history

The misery of fatigue outlines the folds and wrinkles in his grimace

As he lays the premise for his arguments

He raises his rusty blade, and with deliberate motion, he lands his first blow –

You've done this once before, have you yet to learn?

You've felt the pain, and you've hurt those in your concern

But - the younger man, though clearly affected, is quick to retaliate, he says

I've learned from my mistakes, and now a wiser man than before

I've calculated the probabilities of possibilities and these are simply just new opportunities for me

The past is the past, the times of the old are no more – do not hold me to t em

The ancient, he evades the strikes, and with sadness in his eyes – he replies

Quiet son. We both know how much you have to lose.

The bridges you will burn, with the choice you may choose

Insanity is your expectation for a new outcome

Despite the similarity in your situation, this cannot be undone

But un-phased, the youth takes these swings in stride – he says

I am not petty, I am not old, I need not bridges to cross oceans

I am instead ready, and I am yet bold, I can do anything if I have just the notion

Times have changed since then, and it's only fair to me, that I do this

The two desperately look at each other, the old man tired from combat

And the youth now filled with the paralyzing fear of a novice…

The winds continue to blow as walk on… Trying to forget what I've seen

Like a journeyman only just realizes the journeys he has been on

I ponder, and I wonder

To whom, shall victory be awarded? To whom?

Alter Ego (S)

I wish to alter my alter ego, the hero that we know I'll never be though.

But me, yo, I falter with fear of the alter, despite feelin' the vibes of Neyo

Lost in the vast open sea, yo, Nemo. Yet still hooked to the girl, I follow wherever she goes.

Never risk the danger to attempt to change her, re arrange her, make her a stranger. 'Cause -

She the best thing I've ever known, what I've always dreamed to make my own

But the distance is the opponent, and despite my motive, and whether I wrote it, my message to me is all encoded. Its lyrically given, but I lost it, so find it lost in the rhythm

And hear me out, you are what it's about

Map in the Sky (S)

Always on the back of mind, hind brain, my pain comes from what seems her gain,

so, I drift in and out the fast lane

While some love and make movies jealous, I lose mine amid the antics of the fellas,

But things will be different. 'Cause,

I plan to enter the opening a different way,

an audible – a late play. Into the gateway

I don't care what they say

The starry sky is a map of yesterday,

but when I look up I see the future, so ask away

A story of brightness, 'cause clouds are made of condensation

not hesitation. So, me, I'll play it right, to get it right

The jumbled of words in my mind, I'll place em right,

No, you're right, I guess I just, I just might. Take this chance,

'Cause you're like the grid to my maps, the line that fills the gaps

Burdens (S)

Sometimes I wish I had all those happy songs to sing

To shout,

And I've got a lot to say, but somethings I just can't talk about

With each handful of words that come from my mouth,

 I hope a little truth makes its way through to you

Would you still look me in the eyes, if you knew what they've seen?

Still take my heart as yours if you knew where it's been?

Would you still hold my hands if you knew what they've done?

Because as imperfect as I am, they fit so perfectly as one

In Our Closets

I never made a trip home where I didn't look in my closet

I thought I threw away the key, but I never really lost it.

The skeletons are still there, and they continue to haunt me

They are onto me, and taunt me as I walk my path

Introductions

I must meet you, I'm convinced –

I've watched you for a minute, I must admit,

My name is Prince and I'm easily inspired

I'll tell you more about myself, though you haven't inquired

So, give me a listen and show me some love,

That's all that's required

Purple Dark Sky

Purple Dark Sky in my eyes
Laying with a girl I choose to despise

Decent Human Being

Words are but signs

But purpose and reason make plot, not action

Applaud that which permits criticism 'cause

Falling short is tolerated not because it's acceptable

But because it is forgivable.

Draw your parallels towards where you must go,

Or you will get nowhere.

Just be a decent human being.

Mountains and the Sky

As large and commanding as the mountains may be,

As domineering and defeating as they may seem,

their bold attempts to intrude on the sky's tranquility

are fruitless, almost laughable.

Lessons

Climbing does not make us champions.
Rather, the summit humbles us to insignificance.

Man's ability to swim did not allow us to own the seas,
But it taught us humility through our helplessness

Man's ability to fly did not allow us to command the skies
But be taught humility through its expansiveness

Man's ability to think did not give us intellect and pride
But fostered humility by exposure to ignorance.

The more we know, the more we grow - the more we
realize we are so...

Fleeting Beauty

Graffiti will be taken down or painted over

Sandcastles will return to the sea floor

But the lack of permanence adds a perspective

The fleeting nature may prove to be twice as beautiful

Weight of the World

The cane digs into the semi-soft, malleable soil and creates small periods

Ending the sentences created by the man's two feet

The depth of these periods, these breaths between,

Measure the weight of the world.

Billy Blueshoes

Rooftops on the beach,

Emotions and passion,

But good peoples more than anything.

Muffled noises but halcyon words

Emotions abound, love all around

And good homies, nodding to the sounds

Didn't Know

It was easy to say before
I had my own theory, my own beliefs,
I didn't want to think much of it
And I didn't want it to be a big deal
I truly didn't think that it was.

I don't know exactly when it happened
Nor could I specify what changed -
But Mr. Bishop you're better at this than me -
I fooled around and fell in love.

The Sound

Makes me feel the most comfortable
At home, it brightens my mood.
The goodness of the world
Captured in short breaths.

I love when you laugh.

Live in the Music

Live in the music,

Give it a chance through its different melodies

Through patterns and changes

Just don't press next - this can't be it.

Retweets, Reposts, and Copy/Paste

There was a time when you didn't have to express
yourself through other people's thoughts and words.

Your verbs were your own, and if you didn't know how to
say –
you may just never have.

Learning your own voice and personality –
crafting the words that we speak –
so, to not be disingenuous.

Retweet this if you agree.

Sounds of Silence

Sounds of silence

Resilient to the echoes of self-importance

Heard deafeningly loud and clear.

We are Different

We are different, but we are the same

I'm a believer by heart, and you just played the game

You left with amusement and I was left with pain

And to think you were the one screaming my name

Read like a Book

I told you this day would come, where you would realize

I knew it from the start, I knew it from the heart, and I wasn't about to idealize

Yeah, I'm an asshole, easy for you to say

 but you made me feel like one everyday

No injustice in that, you set the bill I had to pay

Okay, so maybe I wasn't the nicest,

But I gave you truth, reality, that's priceless

All joking aside, I'm not the easiest book to read

I understand that, but follow me when I take the lead

I'm not careful, I drop crumbs all along the way

But if you don't pick them up… well that's okay

You were so eager to get at me to share the bedroom

But I need my headroom, my legroom

I'm not done being myself yet.

3 Seconds (S)

My words can come together to paint a vibrant portrait
But inside my mind is an image – A fortress
In a forest of orchids, they're morbid yet gorgeous
And this picture of you will continue to orbit
 my every thought until I meet-uh Mona Lisa from Ibiza
and give you the visa to my heart
3 second smiles last forever in art
I just close my eyes and see what I can't forget

I could paint this canvas with a blindfold
I'll even do it with my eyes closed – just give me a sec
Matter of fact give me 3 for my masterpiece
3 more seconds and it'll be satisfactory
I'll give you something to remember
Something to haunt your every thought until forever
I'll go and pipeline all my nighttime schemes together
3 more seconds is a lifetime of dreams together

Fight Night

Weight made. Gear prepped. Hands wrapped.

I feed myself angry inspiring voices.

Cultivate my motivation and vigor –

develop a wild energy

only to calm it all down when the outside noises rise.

Quiet in my own thoughts and emotion – until

a blow to my face tries to steal my concentration.

My mind breaks, but hurriedly rushes back to home.

He's more tired than I am. Even if he's not... he is.

The bell saves him, it can only stop me.

He's more tired than I am. Even if he's not... he is.

Eraser

Running through my mind, and all I do is chase her
Rub mistakes into the back, white eraser
Maybe one day, I will go and face her, hopefully amaze her
apply protection on my head and maybe erase her
But it don't go down easy, patron no chaser
Caught up in chasing the freedom of free dome

What dynasty, leave me alone
to die, nasty in my own skin, my own home
Kicking back drinking juice, minute maid
But in a minute, I'll be made, in a minute I'll be paid
But what do it count for, one two three, one more

'Cause once more she'll tell me the razor will raise her
Value in existence, life appraiser, become a curtain raiser
But the moment the blade does graze her, red drops blaze
her
As she tries to remove her spots, her stains, with an
eraser.

Anything you do, written on paper
Can be reversed, fixed with an eraser
All that's left of mistakes are faded away
By an eraser.
But life isn't that easy, the faded mistakes are scars
Hidden beneath the flash and their fancy lives, and fancy
cars
Are real people whose daily lives aren't as simple as ours.

Shouting from the Rooftops (S)

I look to the sky and find your eyes

And I know I don't deserve it, I've told my lies

But I'm not just mouthing these words

We are rooftop shouting, the birds

Will hear,

and maybe one day they will hold you dear

And maybe one day I can say it clear

And look you in the eyes as you stand right here

Thief named 'Past'

I met a thief named Past

And he came to me, trying to steal a gift I have been given

The life that I am actively and currently living

And the future I have yet to have written

Greatness

The crafters of my heart, they knew it from the start

I was crafted to be great, then after to be hung

from the rafters with the rest of the masters of the art

Chasing Birds

We used to chase birds, fully knowing we would never catch them.

We wouldn't really know what to do with ourselves if we ever did.

But it still all made sense for some reason.

But I have no fear for the insecurities of insufficiency

Reason isn't always necessary.

What the idle may perceive as fate, see it simply as result

Allow your hesitations to control you no more

Run

Run

Run until you fly

Run until your feet get sore

Then Fly

Fly until your feet soar

Humility

It does not recognize itself

Nor does it recognize its existence

Just the lack of its presence.

You can have it and not know it, but if you are missing it –

it is likely abundantly clear.

Humility, as I so far understand it, is not lowering yourself

or actively raising others.

It is the recognition and awareness that there is far more

value elsewhere.

Panacea

We, as mankind, have created a panacea –

readily available all around the world.

Many know it as the bar.

Not the location, the facility, or the establishment –

but the physical piece of property that sits between the

servers and the patrons.

42 inches tall,
with just enough overhang to cover what we want.

The sturdy wood serves to uphold the weight of all who
lean on it. Just high enough to comfort but not lull

It receives the spilt drinks, sweat, blood and tears – soaks
it all in and we call it character.

The slams of joy, distress, fascination and anger all
accepted and it responds with a warm thud.

Gentle, anxious taps and soft caresses to ease our minds.

It hears all the stories, the complaints, the ideas and the
secrets – but shares with not a soul.

It brings strangers together, it brings friends closer.

Give it a light rap with your hand, to remind it of your
appreciation.

www.ingramcontent.com/pod-product-compliance
Lightning Source LLC
Chambersburg PA
CBHW031542040426
42445CB00010B/654